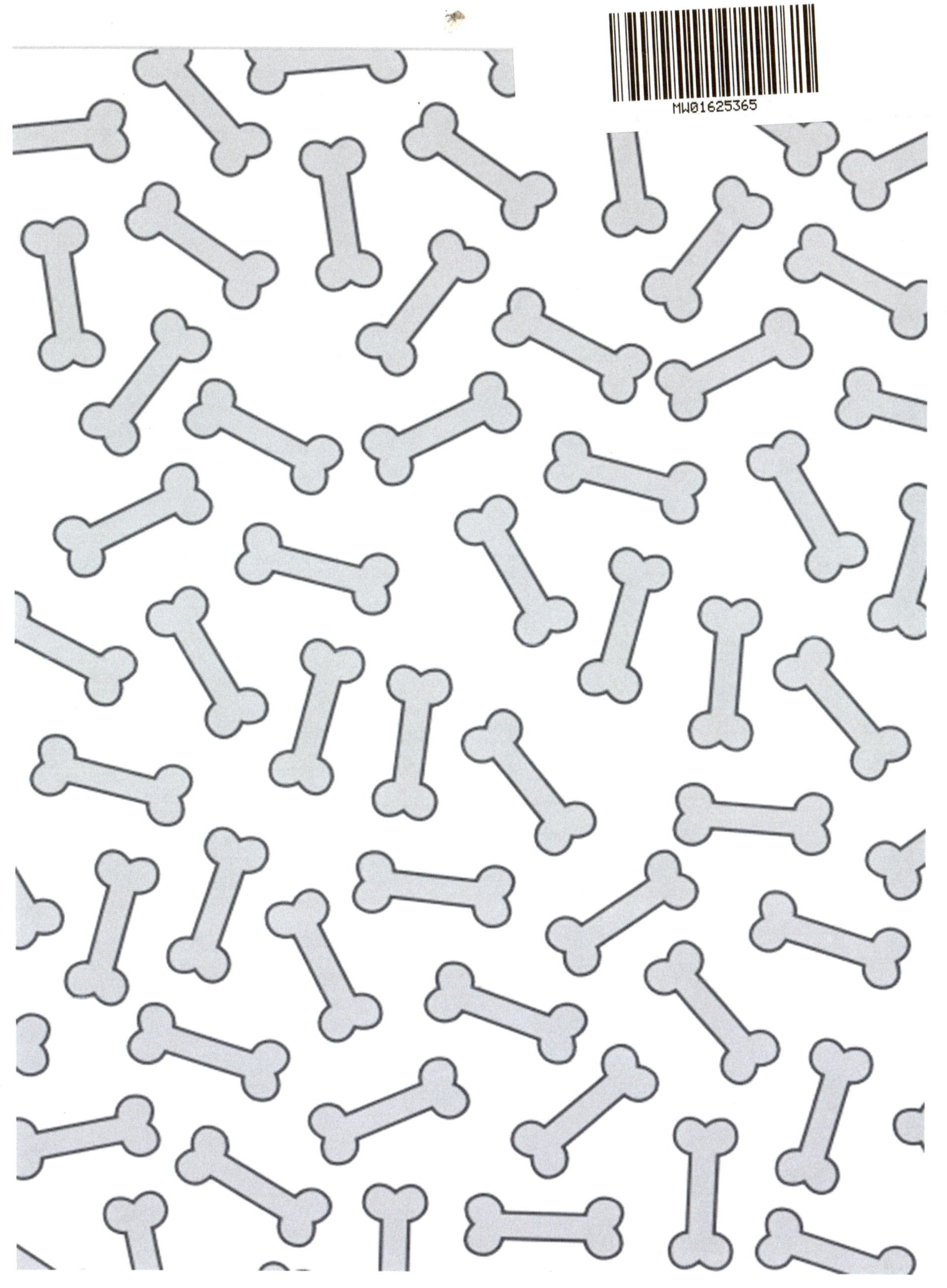

SC

This book is dedicated to the late Dr. Isaiah Reid; my cohort; my nephew, Chris Merrill, #34 on the 2008, 2009, and 2010 MEAC Championship Football Team; the SC State faculty and staff; and my family who encouraged and supported me during my doctoral program at SC State. My career and life have changed for the better since I began in 2000 and graduated in 2004. Forever a loyal daughter.

ISBN 978-0-9980269-7-8

Printed in the United States

OH, TO BE A BULLDOG!

SOUTH CAROLINA STATE
UNIVERSITY

One special fall day,
Dad and Kaidan drove through the gate.
It was Kaidan's first time celebrating
Homecoming at SC State.

SCSU
SCSU

From the little piccolos to the big trombones,
the Marching 101 was working on their line.
Tubas, clarinets, and mighty saxophones
marched, marched, marched in perfect time.

SCSU
SCSU
SCSU

The drums went *Ba-dUm-a-dUm*
while the trombones made a big *hurrah,*
sounding *womp, womp, womp, wommmmmp*
and a *wah, wah, wah, wahhhhhhh.*

SCSU
SCSU

Trumpets played in sync
a very loud *JEEK!* and a honking *TZAAK!*
The flutes joined in playing
buzz, boom, bang, crash, zip, K-LACK!

Dad and Kaidan went to Oliver C. Dawson Stadium
where the team was warming up.
Everyone was happy and smiling,
swallowing tailgate food in big gulps.

The crowd rose as they did the wave
and cheerleaders yelled through megaphones.
Suddenly, an airman landed on the field.
In his hand, an American flag was proudly flown.

Fans went wild as they applauded
for the soldiers and their amazing show.
How had that airman pulled his stunt?
Everybody wanted to know.

The stadium was full
as pom-poms punched the air.
Standing room only!
Not one seat was bare.

101
SCSU
SCSU
SCSU

The dancers pranced back and forth,
as did the Homecoming Court.
Then everyone bowed their heads,
asking that no player be hurt.

Eddie Moe shook hard and rocked,
wowing the crowd on both knees.
The band backed him up
by blaring out "Pass the Peas."

SC STATE
14

"Get your popcorn, candy, peanuts, and Coke,"
yelled the vendor who charged a fee.
Soon it would be time for kickoff
in this huge garnet and blue sea.

Just then, Kaidan noticed Sanchez
after hearing his bark.
SC State's English Bulldog mascot
stood by the fence where his Dad parked.

Dressed in a sweater vest, and pants,
Sanchez was the coolest dog around.
Kaidan couldn't wait until halftime
so he could hit the ground.

Kaidan desired to pet Sanchez
and maybe even shake his paw.
This English Bulldog was so cool,
he left Kaidan in awe.

Dad asked security if Kaidan could pet
the sharp and well-dressed canine.
They gave him permission,
but what was lacking was time.

Kaidan didn't want to leave!
He begged to take Sanchez home.
He didn't have a dog.
As an only child, he was alone.

The game ended, but Kaidan didn't know.
All he could think about was becoming an
owner of his very own English Bulldog.
He'd no longer be a loner.

If Kaidan could show responsibility,
Mom and Dad agreed to buy a pet.
He had to make all A's, clean his room, and do his chores.
It was a lot, but Kaidan's mind was set.

His room clean and chores done,
his report card with straight A's through,
Kaidan was tickled
as they drove to the animal rescue.

There Kaidan saw him,
all fluffy and white.
His own English Bulldog.
It was love at first sight.

Kaidan named the dog "SC."
An excellent name, he knew.
He trained him with much love
and they became an inseparable two!

OH
To Be a Bulldog

In future years, they went to college together,
a mascot and a future engineer.
SC was Kaidan's friend, roommate,
study partner, and peer.

Now a full-fledged pet owner,
Kaidan closed his eyes and began to reminisce.
He thought of the years he'd spent with SC.
His world had become full of bliss.

He remembered the song his mother taught him
when he was three or four.
"Oh, To Be a Bulldog" had new meaning
like it never did before.

SOUTH CAROLINA STATE
UNIVERSITY

"Oh, To Be a Bulldog
will be a dream come true.
Oh, To Be a Bulldog,
it's what I want to do.

Staying focused and studying hard
are a big part of a successful life.
Work hard now and stay committed.
That will surely lessen strife.

Why a Bulldog you might ask,
Wearing garnet and blue?
Not a Tiger, Gamecock, or a Chant?
There's nothing more I'd rather do!

SC State was established in 1896.
MEAC Champs and full of loyalty.
On 300 College Street, Northeast,
a mighty bulldog—there's nothing more I'd
rather be."

Fun Facts About South Carolina State University

Location: Orangeburg, SC (47 miles south of Columbia, SC)

Established: 1896

Colors: Blue and garnet

Mascot: Bulldogs

HBCU: Only South Carolina public historically black college and university.

MEAC: SC State won or shared football titles in the Mid-Eastern Athletic Conference in 2004, 2008, 2009, 2010, and 2013.

Programs: Only Bachelor of Science program in nuclear engineering in SC and at an HBCU.

Only Master of Science degree in transportation and only Master of Business Administration degree with a concentration in agribusiness in SC.

Only Doctor of Education degree in SC with a concentration in educational administration (ranked third Doctor of Education in the nation in graduating minorities with the doctor of education degree).

Alma Mater

Sing the praise of Alma Mater
Let us rally to her call
Lift our voices, send them ringing,
Thru the groves and classic halls.
Hail! Hail! Dear Alma Mater
Hail! Hail! Dear S.C.C.
We'll defend and honor,
Love and cherish thee.

We are loyal sons and daughters
Proud to own the name we bear
For the truth that thou has taught us
Ready all to do and dare.
Hail! Hail! Dear Alma Mater
Hail! Hail! Dear S.C.C.
We'll defend and honor,
Love and cherish thee.

Robert S. Wilkinson
T. D. Phillips - 1927

Acknowledgments

I am grateful to my Creator, my family, SC State, my professors (especially the late Dr. Isaiah Reid), my classmates, and my illustrator, Neel Solanki. I admonish future generations to continue the "Bulldog Strong" legacy.

About the Author

Passionate about creating tomorrow's leaders, Amazon Best Selling Author Dr. Sonia Cunningham Leverette combines her love for children with books. Wife, mother, and veteran educator with almost thirty years of experience, Dr. Leverette focuses extensively on meeting the needs of grade school students.

Her children's books, *BJ's Big Dream, He Never Slumbers, What is That Stinky, Winky Eeewww Smell?* and *My Friends Lived in the Outlet* address self-esteem, self-confidence, and goal-setting. In *Oh, To Be a Bulldog*, Dr. Leverette's love for her alma mater, South Carolina State University, shines through, and her goal is to inspire a desire to attend college within elementary students while highlighting the numerous positive attributes of the school. The author can be contacted via her website, which is BJsBigDream.com.

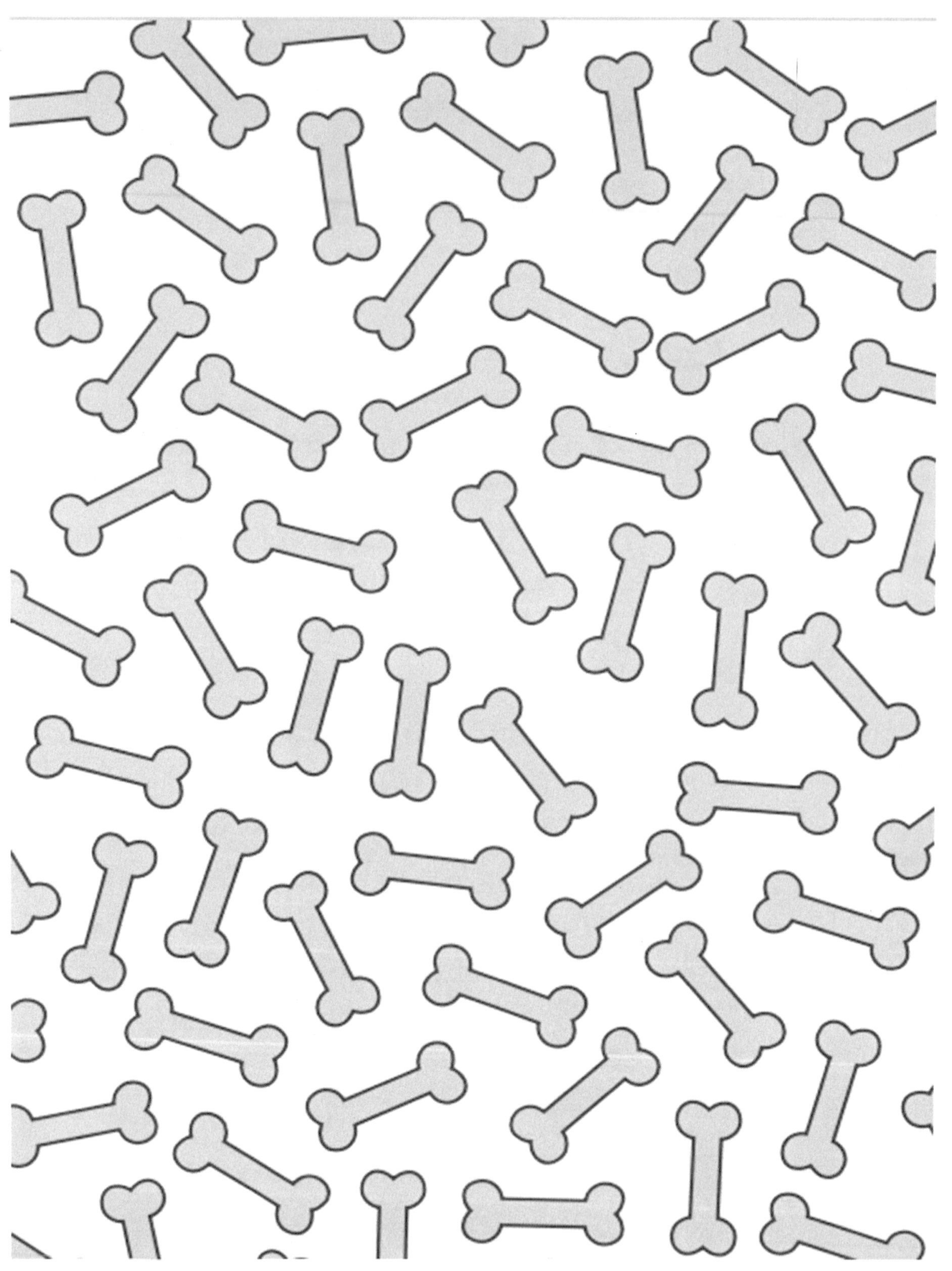

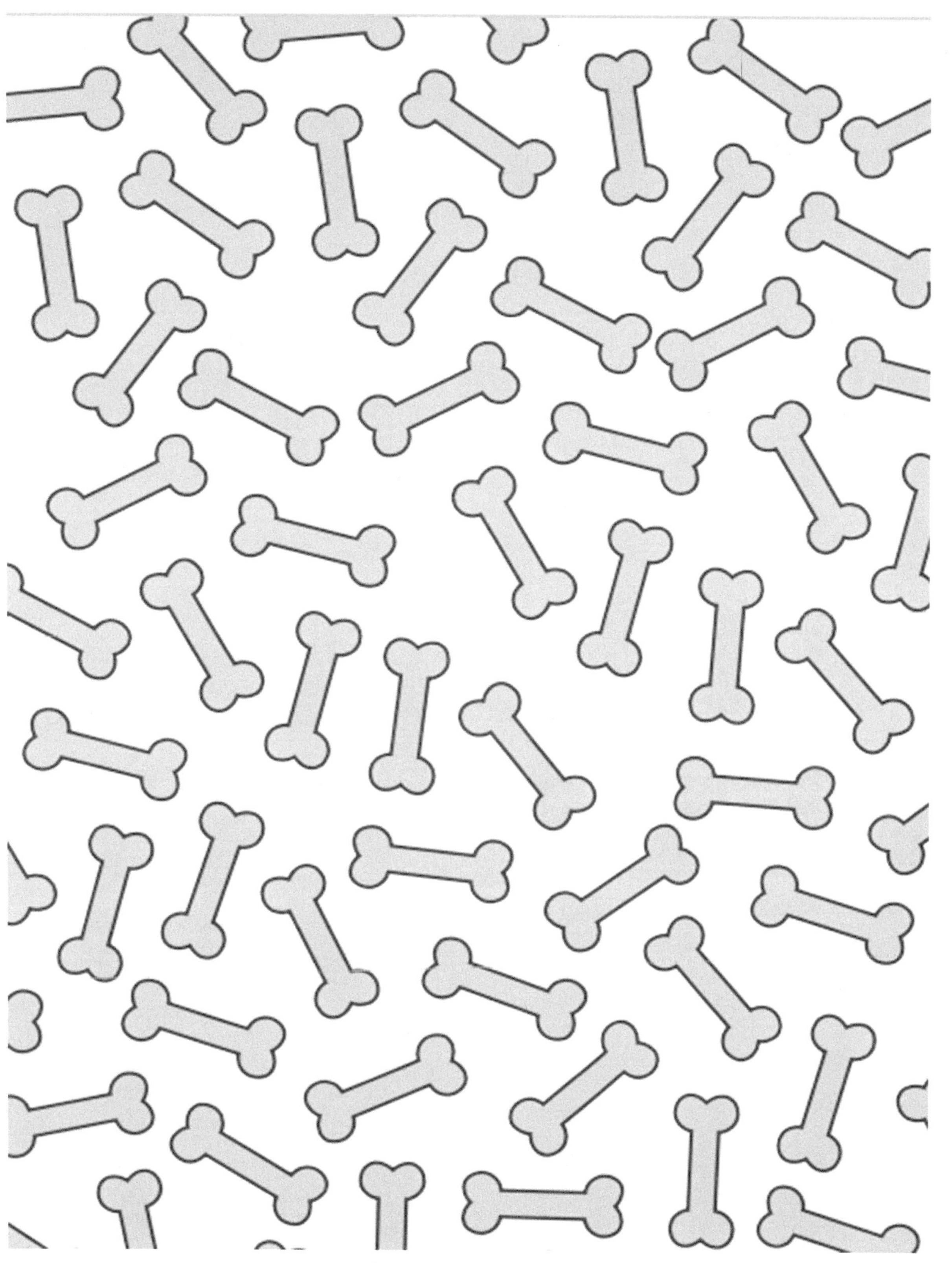

Made in the USA
Columbia, SC
01 May 2021